ANDREW LAI

ISBN 979-8-88540-171-5 (paperback)
ISBN 979-8-88540-173-9 (hardcover)
ISBN 979-8-88540-172-2 (digital)

Christian Faith Publishing
832 Park Avenue
Meadville, PA 16335
www.christianfaithpublishing.com

Printed in the United States of America

I was born in a small town called Kampar (meaning "Golden Treasure") in Malaysia. It is in the state of Perak, which is very rich in tin ore. Not surprising then, my father worked for a British tin-mining company. He was a hard worker and able to teach himself English. He was rewarded with a promotion that required the whole family to be relocated to Kuala Lumpur, where the home office was.

I was about nine years old. Among the moving boxes, I found a pencil drawing of a lion by my father. I was captivated by it. Upon his returning home from work that evening, he was greatly delighted to find my drawing of ten copies of the lion proudly hung on the wall.

That was the beginning of my love for art. In junior high school, my teacher discovered my love for art. In high school, the biology teacher took advantage of my artistic skill. He always assigned me the duty of drawing on the blackboard human organs like the heart, lung, kidney, and so on. Other students would copy my drawing in their notebooks. In the high school biology examination, there was always a question: "Draw a human heart [or other organs]. Name all the vital parts and describe their functions." By the time I graduated from high school, I was a well-liked artist among the teachers and scout-master for doing posters and announcement bulletins.

Unfortunately, my father died of heart attack. My mother had to move me and my two brothers and three sisters to a village to be cared for by our uncle and aunt. She would get a job in the big city to support all of us.

Transferring from Chinese to English school called the Anglo-Chinese Secondary (ACS) School, I needed a tutor to improve my English, but I could not afford one. But a Christian friend's father allowed me to join his tutoring class free of charge. I was able to pass my high school examination, which enabled me to attend college and become a math and science school teacher.

To thank my tutor, I painted a portrait of Jesus for him:

From being a math and science school teacher, I became a cost engineer, chief accountant for a construction company, vice president of another company. All this time, I was active in the First Baptist Church of Richmond, California, and eventually was ordained to be the executive pastor. While pastoring the church, I was able to complete my master's degree from Baptist seminary and also awarded an honorary PhD of divinity by another Christian university. Currently I am retired but still invited to preach in Indonesian and Mien churches.

However, art has never left me. Even though I have never attended art school, I continue to do oil and acrylic paintings. My skill has improved, and I am able to sell some of my paintings to help fund missions in churches and for nonprofit organizations doing social and ministry works in Africa, India, and the Philippines.

Here are a few of my paintings from wildlife, still-life flowers and birds, to landscape.

WILDLIFE

ARTIST APPRECIATION
Presents a Diamond Award To
Andrew Lai
Top 10 Winner of the Deer Contest
Congratulations!!
Gretchen Onstott
Group Administrator
June 2021

Portrait of a male lion

The local people in Zambia recognized this lioness by the birthmark on her neck.

Tiger in lotus pond

Tiger in forest

Tiger cub—what is this?

STILL LIFE, FLOWERS, AND BIRDS

Still life—persimmons from my garden

Hydrangea and Monarch Butterfly

Eagle—the flight above the storm

Those who wait will soar

A pair of mandarin ducks

Wild ducks

Award-winning—A Narrow Escape

The bluebird is one of the most beautiful birds

A pair of cardinals

Lady Amherst's pheasant is one of the most beautiful birds in the world

Hummingbird

Red-crowned cranes—hung in high school library (Yunnan, China)

LANDSCAPES

Bald eagle—three waterfalls

My retirement home

Righteous path is not easy

Lighthouse

ABOUT THE AUTHOR

Rev. Dr. Andrew Lai completed his high school education in the Anglo-Chinese Secondary School, Kampar, Perak, Malaysia. After his college graduation, he became a math and science teacher in Malaysia. After his immigration to San Francisco, he worked as a cost engineer and then became the vice president of a small construction company. All the while, he was teaching an adult Sunday school class in a Baptist church, which eventually ordained him to be the pastor.

While pastoring the church, Andrew attended and graduated from the Golden Gate Baptist Theological Seminary, California. Due to his thirty years of serving the Yiu-Mienh Baptist churches along the West Coast as their conference speaker and youth camp director, he was conferred an honorary PhD of divinity by the Evangel Christian University, Louisiana.

He was married to his wife, Liza, for forty years till she passed away from cancer. Andrew has three children: his son, Daniel, is the associate regional director of Young Life in San Francisco; his daughter, Christina, is a linguist; the youngest daughter, Emily, is an auto mechanic. All three of them are happily married, and each has two young children.